Macmillan/McGraw-Hill Edition

McGRAW-HILL READING

McGRAW-HILL READINESS

McGraw-Hill School Division

A Division of The **McGraw-Hill** Companies

Copyright © 2001 McGraw-Hill School Division, a Division of the Educational and Professional Publishing Group of The McGraw-Hill Companies, Inc.

McGraw-Hill School Division
Two Penn Plaza
New York, NY 10121

Printed in the United States of America

ISBN 0-02-185432-7 / 1

    5 6 7 8 9 071 04 03 02 01 00

**McGraw-Hill
School Division**

New York   Farmington

Table of Contents

1. d

2. t

3. a

4. e

5. b

6. s

7. m

8. p

Look at the letter. • Say the sound it stands for. • Say the picture names. • Circle
the picture whose name begins with the sound that letter stands for.

1.

_____

‑ ‑ ‑ ‑ ‑ ‑ ‑ ‑ ‑ ‑ ‑ ‑ ‑ ‑ ‑
n

_____

2.

_____

‑ ‑ ‑ ‑ ‑ ‑ ‑ ‑ ‑ ‑ ‑ ‑ ‑ ‑ ‑

_____

3.

_____

‑ ‑ ‑ ‑ ‑ ‑ ‑ ‑ ‑ ‑ ‑ ‑ ‑ ‑ ‑

_____

4.

_____

‑ ‑ ‑ ‑ ‑ ‑ ‑ ‑ ‑ ‑ ‑ ‑ ‑ ‑ ‑

_____

5.

_____

‑ ‑ ‑ ‑ ‑ ‑ ‑ ‑ ‑ ‑ ‑ ‑ ‑ ‑ ‑

_____

6.

_____

‑ ‑ ‑ ‑ ‑ ‑ ‑ ‑ ‑ ‑ ‑ ‑ ‑ ‑ ‑

_____

7.

_____

‑ ‑ ‑ ‑ ‑ ‑ ‑ ‑ ‑ ‑ ‑ ‑ ‑ ‑ ‑

_____

8.

_____

‑ ‑ ‑ ‑ ‑ ‑ ‑ ‑ ‑ ‑ ‑ ‑ ‑ ‑ ‑

_____

9.

_____

‑ ‑ ‑ ‑ ‑ ‑ ‑ ‑ ‑ ‑ ‑ ‑ ‑ ‑ ‑

_____

Say each picture name. • What sound does each picture name end with? • Write
the letters that stand for the sound.

Name

1. c a t   cat

2. n e t

3. p i g

4. p o t

5. s u n

Blend the sounds the letters stand for to read the word. • Then write the word.
• Circle the picture that goes with the word.

Name_____

1.

c
(g)

___ c ap

2.

p
b

___ ox

3.

i
o

l ___ ck

4.

e
u

r ___ g

5.

x
j

si ___

6.

m
n

va ___

Say the picture name. • Circle the missing letter. • Then write the letter.
• Read the word.

PRETEST Phonics: Blending

1. has   is   with   (the)

2. he   not   go   a

3. you   that   for   and

4. to   are   do   I

5. of   have   was   said

6. we   my   me   she

Listen to the word. • Circle the word you hear.

1. have ⟨ said ⟩ said

2. we me _____

3. my she _____

4. has he _____

5. the that _____

6. with was _____

Listen to the word. • Circle the word you hear. • Write the word.

Say the name of each picture. • If the name begins with the same sound as *nest*,
write *Nn* on the line.

_n

Name_____

1.  _____

2. _____

 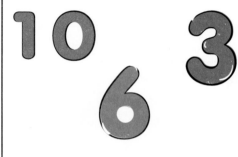

3. _____

4. _____

5. _____

6. _____

Write the letter *n*. • Say the name of each picture. • Draw a line from the *n* to the picture whose name has the same ending sound as *fan*.

	1.	2.
Aa	Aa	

3.	4.	5.

6.	7.	8.

Say the name of each picture. • If the name begins with the same sound as *apple*, write *Aa* on the line.

Name _____

1. _____

2. _____

3. _____

4. _____

5. _____

6. _____
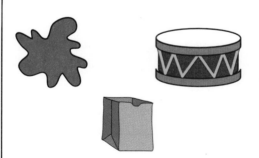

Write the letter. • Say the name of each picture. • Draw a line from the *a* to the picture whose name has the same middle sound as *cat.*

Name_____

1. _____

n

2. _____

n

3. _____

n

4. _____

a

5. _____

a

6. _____

a

Trace the letter. Say the sound it stands for. • Say the names of the pictures.
• Draw a line from the letter to the picture whose name has the sound the letter stands for.

1.

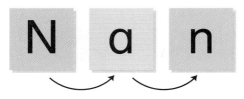 

2.

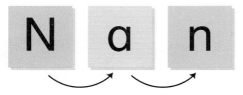

3.

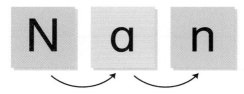

4.

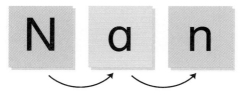

5.

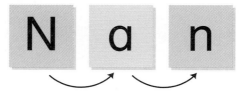

Blend the sounds the letters stand for to read the word. • Trace the letters. • Then
write the word. • Circle the picture that goes with each word.

1. | the | is | (the) | is | the

2. | is | is | the | the | is

3. | is | is | is | the | the

4. | the | the | is | is | the

5. | the | is | the | is | the

Read the first word in each row. • Circle the words in the row that are the same.

1.    is   the

2. is   the

3. is   the

4. the   is

5. is   the

6. is   the

Listen to the word. • Circle the word you hear. • Write the word.

Review High-Frequency Words

Dd	**1.** Dd	**2.**
3.	**4.**	**5.**
6.	**7.**	**8.**

Say the name of each picture. • If the name begins with the same sound as *duck*, write *Dd* on the line.

Name _____

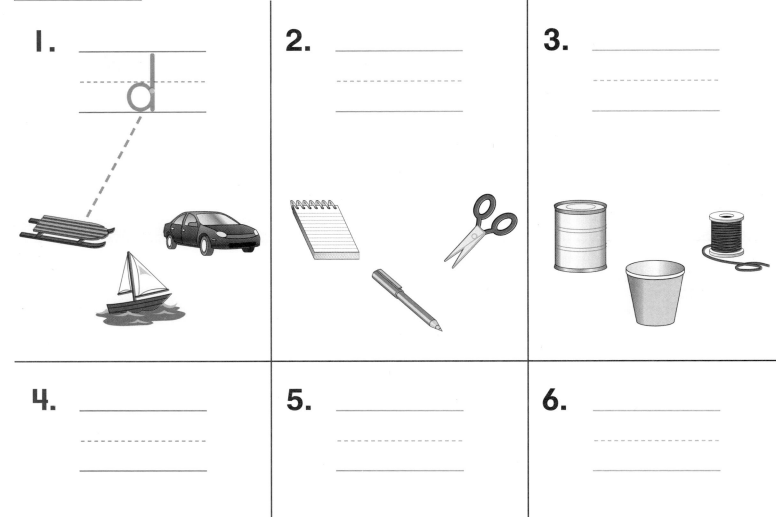

1. _____

2. _____

3. _____

4. _____

5. _____

6. _____

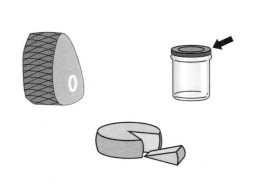

Write the letter *d.* • Say the name of each picture. • Draw a line from the *d* to each picture whose name has the same ending sound as *bed.*

Ss

1.

Ss

2.

3.

4.

5.

6.

7.

8.

Say the name of each picture. • If the name begins with the same sound as *sock*, write *Ss* on the line.

Ss

Name_____

1. _____

2. _____

3. _____

4. _____

5. _____

6. _____
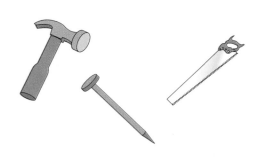

Write the letters *Ss.* • Say the name of each picture. • Draw a line from *Ss* to the picture whose name has the same beginning sound as *sock.*

1. _____

s

2. _____

s

3. _____

d

4. _____

d

5. _____

s

6. _____

d

Trace the letter. • Say the sound it stands for. • Say the names of the pictures.
• Draw a line from the letter to the picture whose name has the sound the letter stands for.

Name_____

1.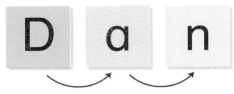

2.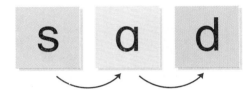

3.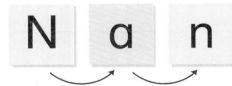

4.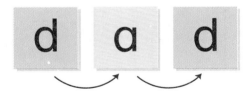

5.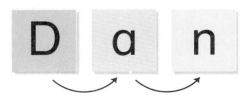

Blend the sounds the letters stand for to read the word. • Trace the letters.
• Then write the word. • Circle the picture that goes with each word.

Blending with Short *a*

McGraw-Hill School Division

Name_____

1.

| with | has | (with) | has | with |

2.

| with | has | with | has | with |

3.

| with | with | with | has | has |

4.

| has | has | with | with | has |

5.

| has | with | has | with | has |

Read the first word in each row. • Circle the words in the row that are the same.

Name_____

1.    is   with

2. the   has

3. with   the

4. has   is

5. with   is

6. is   has

Listen to the word. • Circle the word you hear. • Then write the word.

Name_____

1.

2.

3.

4.

5.

6.

7.

8.

Say the name of each picture. • If the name begins with the same sound as *moon*,
write *Mm* on the line.

Name _____

1. _____

2. _____

3. _____

4. _____

5. _____

6. _____

Write the letter *m*. • Say the name of each picture. • Draw a line from the *m* to each picture whose name has the same ending sound as *drum*.

	1.	2.
I i	I i	

3.	4.	5.

6.	7.	8.
7		

Say the name of each picture. • If the name begins with the same sound as *igloo*, write *Ii* on the line.

_i_

Name_____

1. _____

_i_

2. _____

6 10 4

3. _____

4. _____

5. _____

6. _____

Write the letter *i* on the lines. • Say the name of each picture. • Draw a line from the *i* to the picture whose name has the same middle sound as *pig*.

1. _____
m

2. _____
m

3. _____
m

4. _____
i

5. _____
i

6. _____
i

Trace the letter. Say the sound it stands for. • Say the names of the pictures.
• Draw a line from the letter to the picture whose name has the sound the letter
stands for.

Name _____

1.

M i n

2.

S a m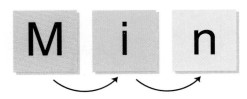

3.

m a n

4.

D a n

5.

N a n

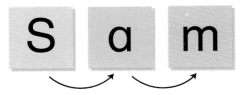
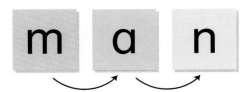
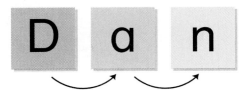
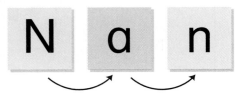

Blend the sounds of the letters together to read the word. • Trace the letters. • Then
write the word. • Circle the picture that goes with each word.

Dad has Sam!

Sam

Sam!

Sam is with Dan.

Sam is with Nan.

Sam?

Sam is with Min.

Sam is with the sad man.

Tt

1. Tt

2.

3. 10

4. 6

5.

6.

7.

8.

Say the name of each picture. • If the name begins with the same sound as *turtle*, write *Tt* on the line.

1.

2.

3.

4.

5.

6.

7.

8.

Say the name of each picture. • If the name has the same ending sound as *hat*, write *t* on the line.

McGraw-Hill School Division

Name

1. _____

2. _____

3. _____

4. _____

5. _____

6. _____

Write the letters *Cc.* • Say the name of each picture. • Draw a line from *Cc* to each picture whose name begins like *cap.*

Name_____

Say the name of each picture. • If the name begins with the same sound as *cap*, write *Cc* on the line.

Name_____

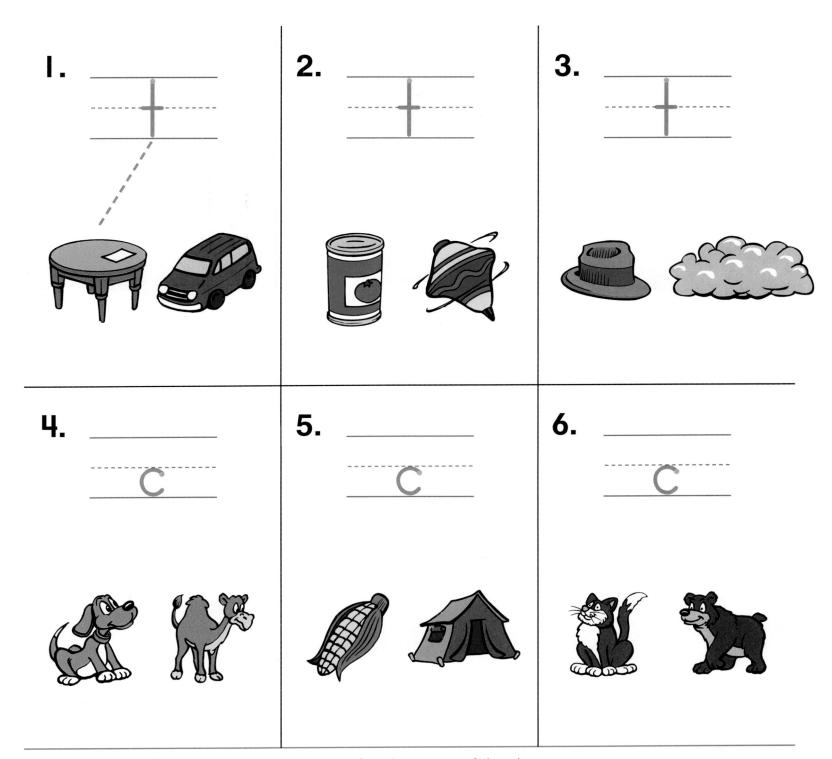

1. t

2. t

3. t

4. c

5. c

6. c

Trace the letter. • Say the sound it stands for. • Say the names of the pictures.
• Draw a line from the letter to the picture whose name has the sound the letter stands for.

Name_____

1.  (cat) can _____ cat

2.  Min Sid _____

3.  cat can _____

4.  man mat _____

5.  sad sit _____

Read the words. • Circle the word that names the picture. • Then write the word.

1.

| he | not | (he) | not | he |

2.

| not | he | not | he | not |

3.

| not | not | he | not | he |

4.

| he | he | not | not | he |

5.

| he | not | he | not | he |

Read the first word in each row. • Circle the words in the row that are the same.

1. (he)　　the　　_he_

2. not　　is

3. has　　with

4. is　　he

5. the　　not

6. has　　with

Listen to the word. • Circle the word you hear. • Then write the word.

McGraw-Hill School Division

	1.	**2.**
Oo	Oo	

3.	**4.**	**5.**

6.	**7.**	**8.**

Say the name of each picture. • If the name begins with the same sound as *octopus*, write *Oo* on the line.

_ O _

Name _____

1. _____

2. _____

3. _____

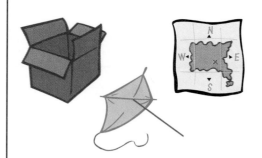

4. _____

5. _____

6. _____

Write the letter *o*. • Say the name of each picture. • Draw a line from the *o* to each
picture whose name has the same middle sound as *pot*.

44   Introduce Medial /o/*o*

	1.	2.
Ff	Ff	

3.	4.	5.

6.	7.	8.

Say the name of each picture. • If the name begins with the same sound as *fish*, write *Ff* on the line.

Ff

Name_____

1.

Ff

2. _____

_____

3. _____

_____

4. _____

_____

5. _____

_____

6. _____

_____

Write the letters *Ff*. • Say the name of each picture. • Draw a line from *Ff* to the picture whose name has the same beginning sound as *fish*.

1.

O   O

2.

o

3.

f

4.

f

Trace the letter. • Say the picture name. • If you hear the sound the letter stands for at the beginning of the picture name, write the letter in the first box. • If you hear the sound in the middle, write the letter in the middle box. • If you hear the sound at the end, write the letter in the last box.

1.

cot
cat

cot

2.

fin
fan

3.

Sam
Nan

4.

man
mad

5.

dad
dot

Read the words. • Circle the word that names the picture. • Then write the word.

Fin the Cat is in!

Tam and Fin

Tam is not sad.

He is not on the cot.

Fin the Cat is not in.

Tam has a tin can.

He is not with Dot.

He is not with Dad.

Name_____

1.

i
(a)

c a t

2.

f
s

__ an

3.

i
o

d __ t

4.

i
a

f __ n

5.

c
t

__ ot

6.

d
t

si __

Say each picture name. • Circle the missing letter. • Then write the letter.
• Read the word.

1.

Sam __is__ sad.

(is)

the

2.

Nan is _____ mad.

with

not

3.

Dan _____ a cat.

has

the

4.

The cat is _____ the man.

with

has

5.

Nan sat on _____ cot.

he

the

Read the sentence. • Then circle the word that completes the sentence. • Write it on the line.

McGraw-Hill School Division

Name_____

1. _____

2. _____

3. _____

4. _____

5. _____

6. _____

Write the letters *Rr*. • Say the name of each picture. • Draw a line from *Rr* to each
picture whose name begins like *rainbow*.

Name_____

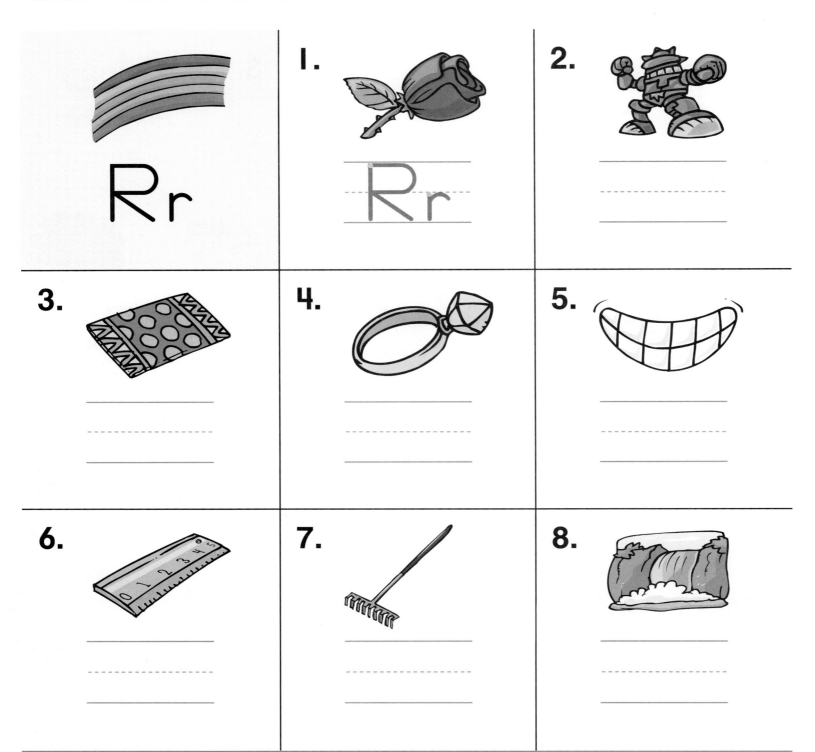

1.

2.

3.

4.

5.

6.

7.

8.

Say the name of each picture. • If the name begins with the same sound as *rainbow,*
write *Rr* on the line.

McGraw-Hill School Division

Name _____

	1.	**2.**
Pp	Pp	_____
3.	**4.**	**5.**
_____	_____	_____
6.	**7.**	**8.**
_____	_____	_____

Say the name of each picture. • If the name begins with the same sound as *pencil*, write *Pp* on the line.

Introduce Initial /p/*Pp*   **55**

Name_____

1.

2.

_p

p

3.

4.

5.

6.

7.

8.

Say the name of each picture. • Write *p* on the line if the name has the same ending sound as *map*.

1.

r

2.

r

3.

p

4.

p

Trace the letter. • Say the picture name. • If you hear the sound the letter stands for at the beginning of the picture name, write the letter in the first box. • If you hear the sound at the end, write the letter in the last box.

1.

~~pot~~ (circled: pot)

pat

p o t

2.

cap

cat

3.

rip

tap

4.

sat

mat

5.

Tom

top

Read the words. • Circle the word that names the picture. • Then write the word.

1.

| and | (and) | you | a | and |

2.

| you | and | you | and | you |

3.

| a | a | and | you | a |

4.

| you | you | and | a | you |

5.

| and | and | you | a | and |

Read the first word in each row. • Circle the words in that row that are the same.

Name_____

1. $\quad$ (and) $\qquad$ a $\qquad$ and

2. $\quad$ you $\qquad$ the

3. $\quad$ has $\qquad$ and

4. $\quad$ a $\qquad$ has

5. $\quad$ you $\qquad$ with

6. $\quad$ the $\qquad$ and

Listen to the word. • Circle the word you hear. • Then write the word.

McGraw-Hill School Division

Name _____

1. _____

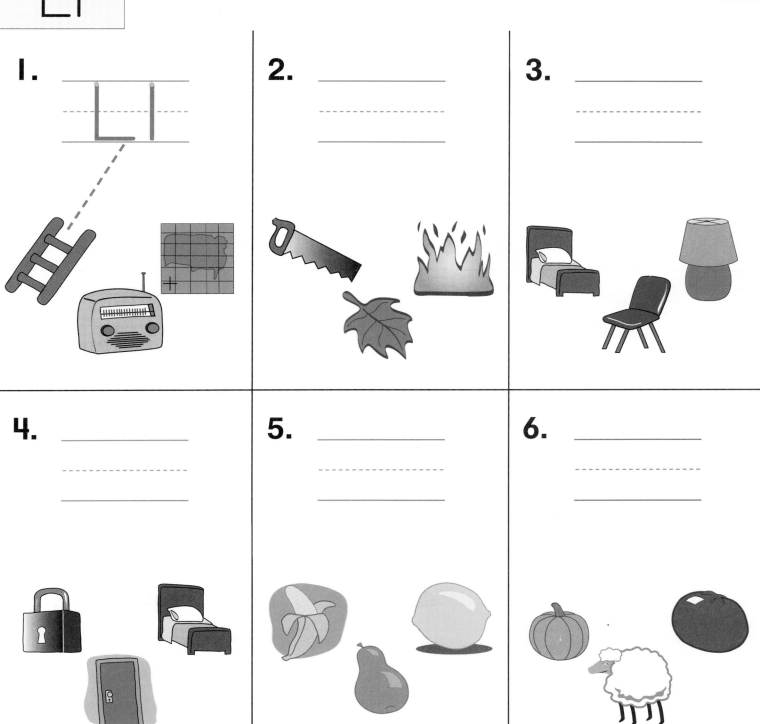

2. _____

3. _____

4. _____

5. _____

6. _____

Write the letters *Ll.* • Say the name of each picture. • Draw a line from *Ll* to each picture whose name begins like *lion.*

3.

4.

5.

6.

7.

8.

Say the name of each picture. • If the name begins with the same sound as *lion*, write *Ll* on the line.

Name_____

Uu

1. Uu

2.

3.

4.

5.

6.

7.

8.

Say the name of each picture. • If the name begins with the same sound as *umbrella,*
write *Uu* on the line.

__u__

Name_____

1. _____

u

2. _____

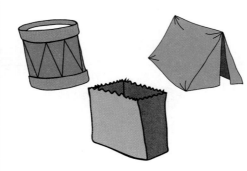

3. _____

4. _____

5. _____

6. _____

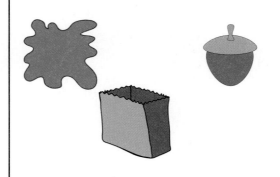

Write the letter *u*. • Say the name of each picture. • Draw a line from the *u* to each picture whose name has the same middle sound as *sun*.

Name

1. l

2. l

3. l

4. u

5. u

6. u

Trace the letter. • Say the sound it stands for. • Say the names of the pictures.
• Draw a line from the letter to the picture whose name has the same sound as the letter.

Review /l/l, /u/u **65**

1.

 u

a

n u t

2.

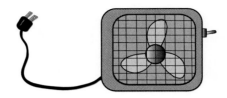

c

f

___ an

3.

p

d

mu ___

4.

n

m

su ___

5.

i

o

p ___ t

6.

l

f

___ ip

Say each picture name. • Circle the missing letter. • Then write the letter. • Read the word.

1. that | for   (that)   go   that

2. for | that   for   for   go

3. go | for   go   that   go

4. for | for   go   that   for

5. that | that   go   that   for

Read the first word in each row. • Circle the words in that row that are the same.

1.

and   (that)   that

2.

you   go

3.

has   for

4.

that   and

5.

you   for

6.

go   a

Listen to the word. • Circle the word you hear. • Then write the word.

Name_____

1. _____

K k

2. _____

3. _____

4. _____

5. _____

6. _____

Write the letters *Kk*. • Say the name of each picture. • Draw a line from *Kk* to each picture whose name begins like *kite*.

Kk

1.

Kk

2.

3.

4.

5.

6.

7.

8.

Say the name of each picture. • If the name begins with the same sound as *kite,*
write *Kk* on the line.

_ck

Name_____

1. _____

ck

2. _____

3. _____

4. _____

5. _____

6. _____

Dear Mom,
Camp is
great!
I miss you!
Love,
Sam

Write the letters *ck.* • Say the name of each picture. • Draw a line from *ck* to each
picture whose name has the same ending sound as *lock.*

__ck

1.

ck

2.

3.

4.

5.

6.

7. 5

8.

Say the name of each picture. • If the name ends with the same sound as *lock*, write *ck* on the line.

1. k

2. k

3. k

4. ck

5. ck

6. ck

Trace the letter or letters. • Say the sound they stand for. • Say the names of the pictures. • Draw a line from the letter or letters to the picture whose name has the same sound.

1.

u

i

c u p

2.

ck

t

du ____

3.

o

i

k ___ ck

4.

m

r

___ op

5.

s

n

fa ___

6.

r

t

___ od

Say each picture name. • Circle the missing letter or letters. • Then write the letter or letters. • Read the word.

A pup can pick Rod and Kit!

A Pup for Rod and Kit

That pup can lick and lick.

That tan pup can sit up.

Rod and Kit can go
pick up a pup.

Can you pick a pup
for Rod and Kit?

That pup can run.

That pup can fit in a pack.

Gg

Name_____

1. _____

Gg

2. _____

3. _____

4. _____

5. _____

6. _____

Write the letters *Gg.* • Say the name of each picture. • Draw a line from *Gg* to each picture whose name begins like *gift.*

1.

g

2.

3.

4.

5.

6.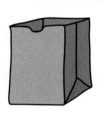

7.

8.

Say the name of each picture. • If the name ends with the same sound as *frog*, write *g* on the line.

	1.	2.
E e	**E e**	
3.	4.	5.
6.	7.	8.

Say the name of each picture. • If the name begins with the same sound as *egg,*
write *Ee* on the line.

Name _____

1. _____

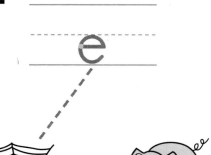

2. _____

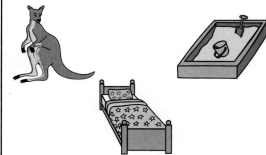

3. _____

4. _____

5. _____

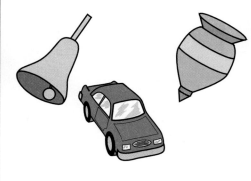

6. _____

Write the letter *e*. • Say the name of each picture. • Draw a line from the *e* to each
picture whose name has the same middle sound as *net*.

1.

g

g

2.

g

3.

e

4.

e

Trace the letter. • Say the picture name. • If you hear the sound the letter stands for at the beginning of the picture name, write the letter in the first box. • If you hear the sound in the middle, write the letter in the middle box. • If you hear the sound at the end, write the letter in the last box.

Name_____

1.  u o

r u n

2.  i e

n _ t

3.  r s

_ un

4.  g f

pi _

5.  p d

to _

6. s t

_ ack

Say each picture name. • Circle the missing letter. • Then write the letter. • Read the word.

Name_____

1.	to	do	(to)	are	to
2.	are	to	do	are	are
3.	do	do	are	to	do
4.	are	are	to	are	to
5.	to	do	are	to	to

Read the first word in each row. • Circle the words in that row that are the same.

Name_____

1.

and		are

2.

| to | go | |

3.

| do | for | |

4.

| are | and | |

5.

| do | for | |

6.

| to | you | |

Listen to the word. • Circle the word you hear. • Then write the word.

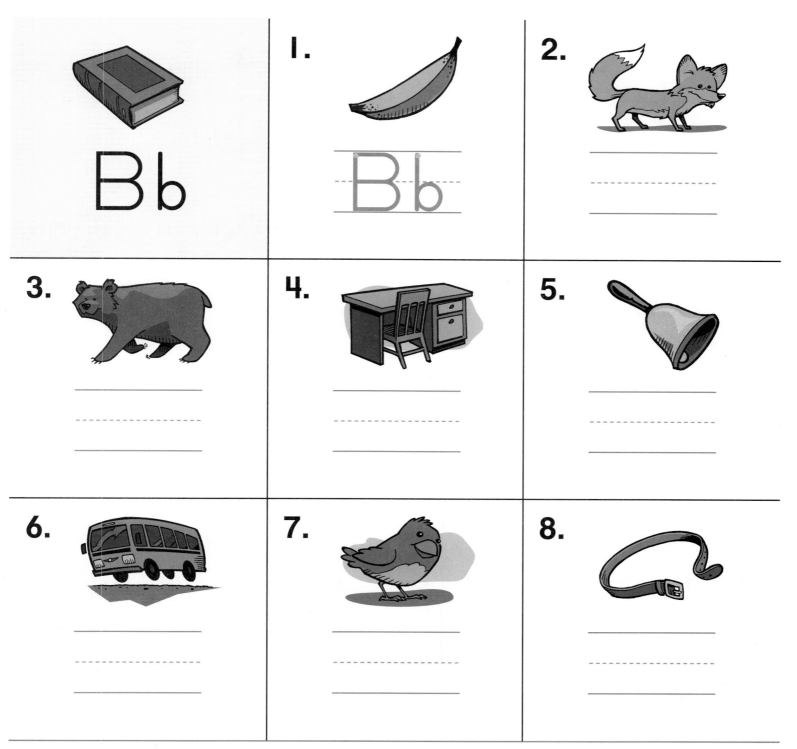

Bb

1. Bb

2.

3.

4.

5.

6.

7.

8.

Say the name of each picture. • If the name begins with the same sound as *book*, write *Bb* on the line.

_b

Name_____

1. _____

b

2. _____

3. _____

4. _____

5. _____

6. _____

Write the letter *b*. • Say the name of each picture. • Draw a line from the *b* to each picture whose name has the same ending sound as *tub*.

1.

2.

3.

4.

5.

6.

7.

8.

Say the name of each picture. • If the name begins with the same sound as *hen*, write *Hh* on the line.

Name_____

1.
Hh

2. _____

3. _____

4. _____

5. _____

6. _____

Write the letters *Hh*. • Say the name of each picture. • Draw a line from *Hh* to each picture whose name has the same beginning sound as *hen*.

1.

h

2.

b

3.

h

4.

b

Trace the letter. • Say the picture name. • If you hear the sound the letter stands for at the beginning of the picture name, write the letter in the first box. • If you hear the sound at the end, write the letter in the last box.

1.

(b)
h

b̲ at

2.

u
i

l ___ ck

3.

s
r

___ ug

4.

f
g

le ___

5.

e
o

p ___ n

6.

m
t

do ___

Say the picture name. • Circle the missing letter. • Then write the letter.
• Read the word.

Ben has to get his hat and his rod.

Do not let go of the rod!

Ben and Gab hop on the log.

It is hot, hot, hot!

That is a big cod!

The Big Tug

Ben has a big tug.

Ben and Gab are set to go.

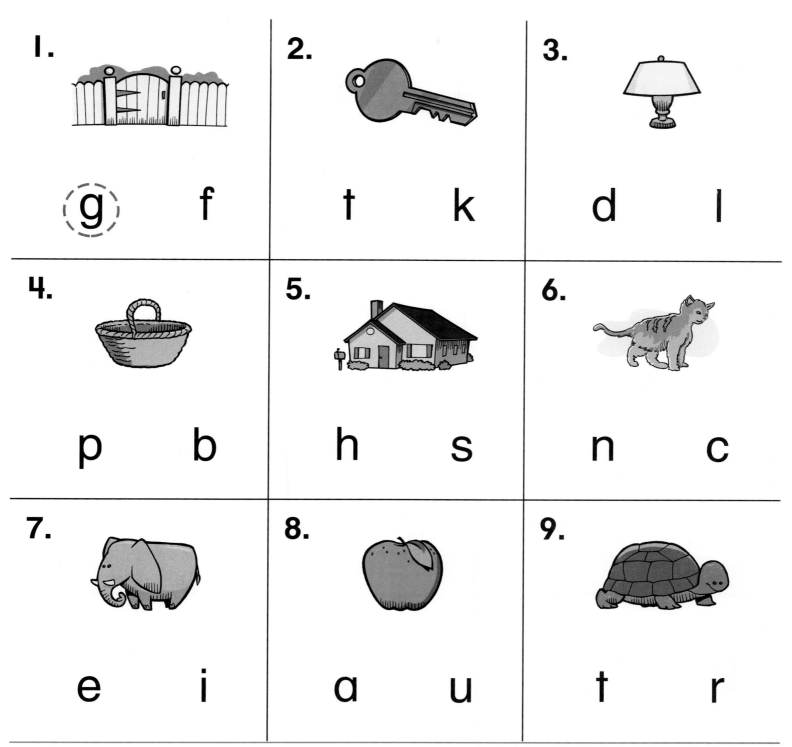

1. g f

2. t k

3. d l

4. p b

5. h s

6. n c

7. e i

8. a u

9. t r

Say each picture name. • Circle the letter that stands for the beginning sound.

1.

Did Dan __go__ to bed?

(go)

are

2.

The bag is _____ you.

that

for

3.

The dog _____ cat can run.

and

to

4.

Kit can _____ it!

you

do

5.

Dad has _____ map.

to

a

Read the sentence. • Then circle the word that completes the sentence. • Write the word on the line.

McGraw-Hill School Division

Name_____

1.

Ww

2.

3.

4.

5.

6.

7.

8.

Say the name of each picture. • If the name begins with the same sound as *wagon*, write *Ww* on the line.

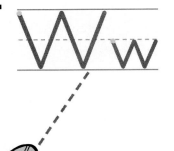

Ww

Name_____

1.

2. _____

3. _____

4. _____

5. _____

6. _____

Write the letters *Ww*. • Say the name of each picture. • Draw a line from *Ww* to each picture whose name has the same beginning sound as *wagon*.

Name_____

	1.	2.
V v	V v	
3.	4.	5.
6.	7.	8.

Say the name of each picture. • If the name begins with the same sound as *vest*, write *Vv* on the line.

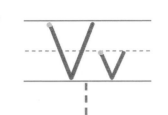

Name_____

1. _____

2. _____

3. _____

4. _____

5. _____

6. _____

Write the letters *Vv*. • Say the name of each picture. • Draw a line from *Vv* to each picture whose name begins like *vest*.

1. _____

W

2. _____

V

3. _____

W

4. _____

V

5. _____

W

6. _____

V

Trace the letter. • Say the sound it stands for. • Say the names of the pictures.
• Draw a line from the letter to the picture whose name begins with the sound the letter stands for.

1.

(b)
t

we b

2.

u
e

b __ s

3.

c
d

__ ot

4.

v
p

__ an

5.

p
d

mo __

6.

o
a

c __ t

Say the picture name. • Circle the missing letter. • Then write the letter.
• Read the word.

1.	of	was	I	(of)	of
2.	I	I	was	I	of
3.	was	I	was	I	was
4.	of	was	I	of	of
5.	was	was	of	was	of

Read the first word in each row. • Circle the words in the row that are the same.

Name _____

I.   a   (I)   I

2.   has   was   _____

3.   of   for   _____

4.   that   was   _____

5.   I   for   _____

6.   go   of   _____

Listen to the word. • Circle the word you hear. • Then write the word.

Name

	1.	2.
_X	X	
3.	4.	5.
6.	7.	8.

Say the name of each picture. • If the name ends with the same sound as *box*,
write *x* on the line.

Name_____

1. _____

2. _____

3. _____

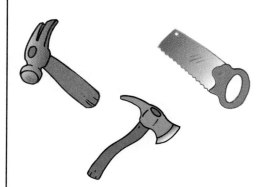

4. _____

5. _____

6. _____

$6 \ 10 \ 4$

Write the letter *x*. • Say the name of each picture. Draw a line from the *x* to each picture whose name has the same ending sound as *box*.

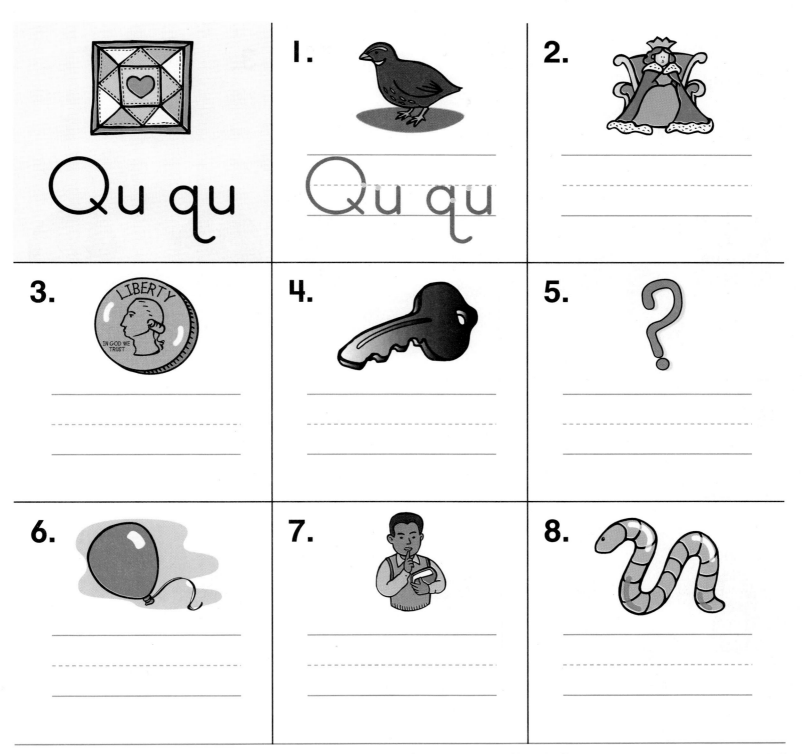

	1.	2.
Qu qu	Qu qu	
3.	4.	5.
6.	7.	8.

Say the name of each picture. • If the name begins with the same sound as *quilt,*
write *Qu,qu* on the line.

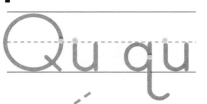

Qu qu Name_____

1. _____

Qu qu

2. _____

_____

3. _____

_____

4. _____

_____

5. _____

_____

6. _____

_____

Write the letters *Qu,qu.* • Say the name of each picture. • Draw a line from *Qu,qu* to each picture whose name has the same beginning sound as *quilt.*

Name_____

1. _____

2. _____

3. _____

4. _____

5. _____

6. _____

Trace the letter or letters. Say the sound they stand for. • Say the names of the
pictures. • Draw a line from the letter or letters to the picture whose name has the
same sound the letter or letters stand for.

Name _____

1. 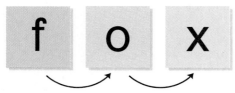   fox

2. 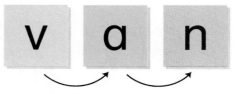   _____

3. 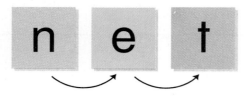   _____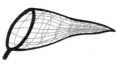

4. 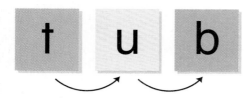   _____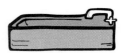

5. 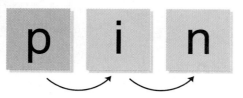   _____

First, blend the sounds and say the word. • Next, write the word. • Last, draw a circle around the picture that goes with the word.

Name_____

1. we	said	(we)	have	we
2. said	have	said	we	said
3. have	have	said	we	have
4. said	said	we	said	have
5. we	we	said	we	have

Read the first word in each row. • Circle the words in the row that are the same.

I. (have) has   have

2. was   we

3. said   do

4. we   of

5. said   I

6. was   have

Listen to the word. • Circle the word you hear. • Then write the word.

Name

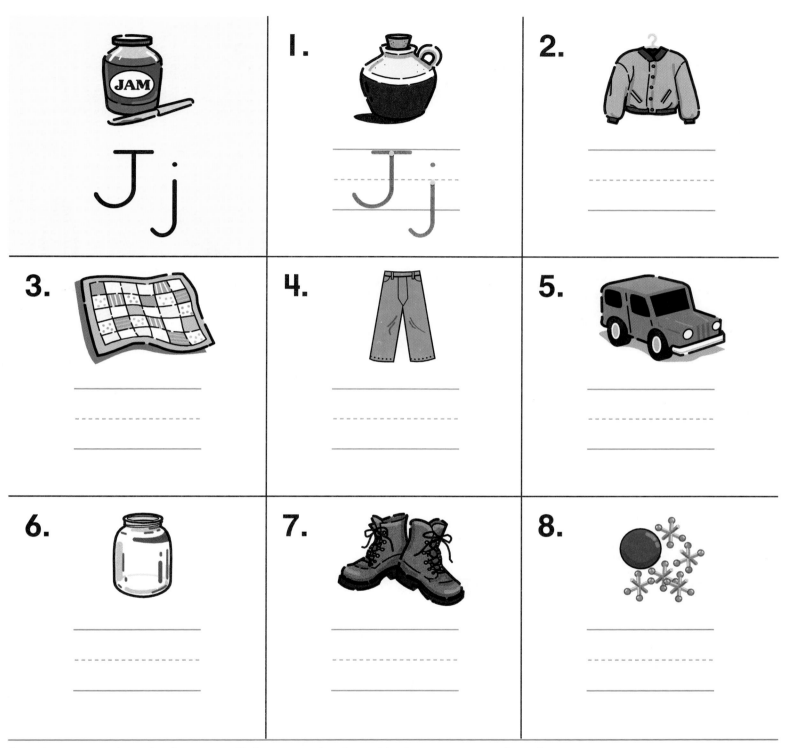

| | 1. | 2. |
| J j | J j | |

| 3. | 4. | 5. |

| 6. | 7. | 8. |

Say the name of each picture. • If the name begins with the same sound as *jam*, write *Jj* on the line.

J j

Name

1. _____

J j

2. _____

3. _____

4. _____

5. _____

6. _____

Write the letters *Jj*. • Say the name of each picture. • Draw a line from *Jj* to each picture whose name has the same beginning sound as *jam*.

Name_____

| | 1. | 2. |

| 3. | 4. | 5. |

| 6. | 7. | 8. |

Say the name of each picture. • If the name begins with the same sound as *yo-yo*,
write *Yy* on the line.

Name _____

1. _____

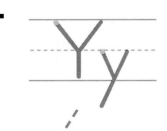

2. _____

3. _____

4. _____

5. _____

6. _____

Write the letters *Yy*. • Say the name of each picture. • Draw a line from *Yy* to each picture whose name has the same beginning sound as *yo-yo*.

Name

1. _____
y

2. _____
j

3. _____
y

4. _____
j

5. _____
j

6. _____
y

Trace the letter. • Say the sound it stands for. • Say the names of the pictures. •
Draw a line from the letter to the picture whose name has the same sound as the letter.

Name_____

1.

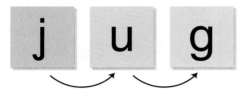

j u g

jug

2.

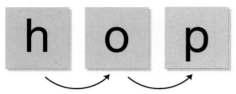

h o p

3.

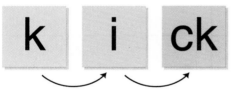

k i ck

4.

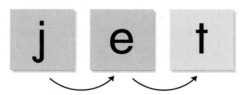

j e t

5.

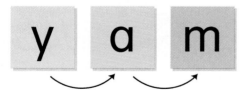

y a m

First, blend the sounds and say the word. • Next, write the word. • Last, draw a
circle around the picture that goes with the word.

"I got a run!" said Jan.
"We win!"

Jan at Bat

Max had to run to pick it up.

"We can win if we get a hit,"
said Yan.

"We have to get a run," said Vick.

2

Jan was quick.

7

Jan got up to bat and got a big hit.

4

Max was at the back of the lot.

5

Name_____

1.

2.

3.

4.

5.

6.

7.

8.

Say the name of each picture. • If the name begins with the same sound as *zipper,*
write *Zz* on the line.

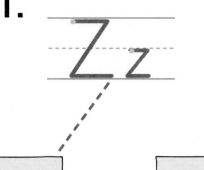

Zz

Name_____

1.

_Zz_

0   1   5

2. _____

 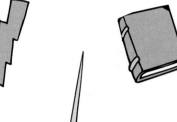

3. _____

4. _____

5. _____

6. _____

 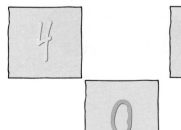

Write the letters _Zz_. • Say the name of each picture. • Draw a line from _Zz_ to each picture whose name has the same beginning sound as _zipper._

1.

y   d

2.

3.

4.

5.

6.

Say the picture name. • Write the letters that stand for the beginning and ending sounds in each picture name.

1.

b	u	g

2.

3.

4.

Say the picture name. • Write the letters that stand for the beginning, middle and ending sounds in the boxes. • Then read the word.

1.

e   g

2.

3.

4.

5.

6.

Say the picture name. • Write the letters that stand for the beginning and ending sounds in each picture name.

Name_____

1.

(e)
a

w e b

2.

i
o

f __ x

3.

o
u

d __ ck

4.

a
i

c __ n

5.

6

e
i

s __ x

6.

a
i

c __ t

Say the picture name. • Circle the missing letter. • Then write the letter.
• Read the word.

Blending with Short *a, i, o, u,* and *e*

Name_____

1.

me | she | (me) | my | me

2.

she | my | me | she | she

3.

my | me | my | she | my

4.

she | she | my | she | me

5.

my | my | me | she | my

Read the first word in each row. • Circle the words in the row that are the same.

Name_____

1.  I   my

2. she   said

3. my   me

4. said   she

5. me   of

6. is   my

Listen to the word. • Circle the word you hear. • Then write the word.

Name_____

1. n

n

2. t

3. z

4. j

5. m

6. a

Look at the letter. • Say each picture name. • Write the letter on the first line if you hear the sound for the letter at the beginning of the word. • Write the letter on the second line if you hear the sound at the end of the word.

1.

cat

cap

cat

2.

lock

kick

3.

fox

hot

4.

tub

pup

5.

him

hen

Read the words. • Circle the word that names the picture. • Then write the word.

1.

(u)

a

s ___ n

s u n

2.

g

b

___ ed

3.

j

g

pi ___

4.

o

a

s ___ ck

5.

f

w

___ eb

6.

n

v

ca ___

Say the picture name. • Circle the missing letter. • Then write the letter.
• Read the word.

Name_____

1. _____

Sam is my pal.

(my)
she

---

2. _____

We _____ a big dog.

have
of

---

3. _____

Mom _____ , "Go to bed!"

was
said

---

4. _____

_____ is up at bat.

Was
She

---

5. _____

Kim _____ at the top.

was
have

Read the sentence. • Then circle the word that completes the sentence. • Write the word on the line.

McGraw-Hill School Division

Name_____

1. _____

Can ___you___ fix it?

you

has

2. _____

Sid _____ Tam are wet.

was

and

3. _____

Pam _____ a red hat.

is

has

4. _____

_____ can go!

Are

We

5. _____

_____ is a big cat!

The

That

Read the sentence. • Then circle the word that finishes the sentence. • Write the word on the line.

Name _____

1. _____
 I have a pet.

(**I**)
he

2.
Pop said we can _____ .

go
a

3.
Can I run _____ you?

go
with

4. _____
_____ can pack the box.

He
Go

5.
The pig _____ in the pen.

is
to

Read the sentence. • Then circle the word that completes the sentence. • Write the
word on the line.

Pam is not big, but she
is a quick kid.

2

She has a big hug for me.

7

She can zig zag up
to the top and back.

4

I run and run, but
I can not win.

5

If I run with Pam
I can get quick!

A Run with Pam

Pam can not let me quit.

She can go with my Mom
and me on a run.

Name _____

Write a message to a friend or family member. ● Remember to write from left-to-right and from top-to-bottom.

Name _____

Write a message to a friend or family member. ● Remember to write from left-to-right and from top-to-bottom.

is	the
not	he
with	has

and

go

a

that

for

you

to

are

do

we

have

said

of

was

I

my

she

me